811.54 S222o
Sandy, Stephen
Overlook : poems

OVERLOOK

WITHDRAWN

BOOKS BY STEPHEN SANDY

POEMS

Overlook, 2010

Netsuke Days, 2008

Weathers Permitting, 2005

Octave (alternately, *Surface Impressions*), 2002

Black Box, 1999

The Thread: New and Selected Poems, 1998

Thanksgiving over the Water, 1994

Man in the Open Air, 1988

Riding to Greylock, 1983

End of the Picaro, 1977

Roofs, 1971

Stresses in the Peaceable Kingdom, 1967

PROSE

The Raveling of the Novel: Studies in Romantic Fiction, 1980

TRANSLATIONS

Aeschylus, *Seven Against Thebes*, 1998

Seneca, *A Cloak for Hercules* (*Hercules Oetaeus*), 1995

Overlook

poems

Stephen Sandy

Louisiana State University Press
Baton Rouge

CUYAHOGA COMMUNITY COLLEGE
EASTERN CAMPUS LIBRARY

Published by Louisiana State University Press
Copyright © 2010 by Stephen Sandy
All rights reserved
Manufactured in the United States of America
LSU Press Paperback Original
First printing

Designer: Laura Roubique Gleason
Typeface: Arno Pro
Printer and binder: McNaughton & Gunn, Inc.

LIBRARY OF CONGRESS CATALOGING-IN-PUBLICATION DATA

Sandy, Stephen.
 Overlook : poems / Stephen Sandy.
  p. cm.
 ISBN 978-0-8071-3692-8 (pbk. : alk. paper)
 I. Title.
 PS3569.A52O94 2011
 811'.54—dc22

2010002510

All etchings are reproduced by permission of the artist, Willard Boepple.

Thanks to Chard deNiord, John Easterly, Ted Gilley, Grey Gowrie, Jen Hinst-White, Richard Howard, Malcolm Hyman, Bill Morgan, Geoffrey Movius, F. D. Reeve, and Mary Ruefle.

Grateful acknowledgment is made to the editors of the following publications, in which many of these poems first appeared: *Agni, Alembic, Atlantic Monthly, Denver Quarterly, Green Mountains Review, Harvard Review, Mudfish, Paris Review, Partisan Review, Per Contra, Poetry London, Raintown Review, The Reader* (UK), *Salamander, Salmagundi, The Southern Review, Times Literary Supplement, Western Humanities Review, Yaddo News, Yale Review.* "Feed the World" first appeared in *For New Orleans,* ed. Ashis Gupta (Bayeux Arts, 2007). "Side Hill Farm" first appeared in *Glastenbury: The History of a Vermont Ghost Town,* by Tyler Resch (History Press, 2007). "Breaking Story" was first published as a broadside by Out of Hand Press.

The paper in this book meets the guidelines for permanence and durability of the Committee on Production Guidelines for Book Longevity of the Council on Library Resources. ∞

For V

CONTENTS

OVERLOOK

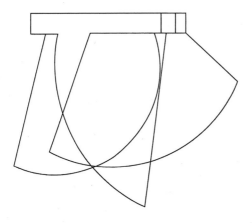

Waxwings

How bold to step into the torrent. Kayakers
shout to him on the bank as they shoot by. A brown
dove under the feeder sorts seeds from snow.

The bass of doubt has slipped its weir, holds steady
against the current. There in the shadowed valley
it is like trying to pull as the lady said

a piano out of a swamp. Then looking up
at the past each night he wonders. He counts hundreds,
thousands but nothing is there. A dropped cell phone

still ringing on a bed of reeds. He falls
on ice but his hand saves him, a fist in the face.
The bruise to come. The crabapple tree is alive

with cedar waxwings, titmice, stripping it. Soon
the plump first robins of spring; they peck and stare
at a few fruits that hung the winter through

and now have fallen, wizened berries of survival.
What can he do back from the stream's loud bank
but keep his eye on the clouds, carry on.

Where Are You Going with That Wrench

A switch went and is going to take up the trip.
Jiggle the handle, engineers! Getting out of the train
to fix it yourselves? Be serious. We have
some promises to keep here. We tick toward night
with cell-phone jitters; but it's not going anywhere.
Snoozes may bowl a dream but no strikes. I prefer
the sensual contours of the bridge off there—
how like your thigh. But after all it's only a bridge

to Hawaii. They are not handing out pillows and should be
putting APB's out on this, our breakdown, the just
sitting here watching lily pads spread over the inlet
of the river where tide and current—forget them, they're
too slight to move a reed. Better to listen to the good people
complain to their cell phones. You'll catch the anxiety the loud
talk. It has not moved. Yet don't we know it's bound
for the Styx? Better to think of existence inside rock; the life

over there for example inside that Palisade, its scree
crumbling down past gulls to the shore where
nearby someone is jet-skiing today, back
and forth wheeling to and fro in the sun, buffing
the glassine surface of the still reach
of light-rimmed river—in slow wide turns
beyond the window that seals us from
the tiny make-believe roar.

Breaking Story

Sort pieces, work the edges, it
becomes a happy endless game.
We wonder why, only a little
why we do it. Still . . .
fascination returns, returns
after you have gone to the kitchen
for the snack you promised yourself
you would wait till eleven for
maybe we look into *The Times*
but only see the full-page spreads
the thin bodies with marvelous jobs
not much of interest beyond
the remote and microscopic chance
of meeting one of them or
becoming one of their happy pack.
The sly temptation comes back

like a miniature addiction—
fit for a dollhouse. Merely fit
one more piece in its proper place
that piece will open all of it up,
key to the whole picture with
its rounded sockets shaggy commas
protrusions like stiffened nipples.
We know there's got to be a scheme
a big picture—but how? A tiny
version—a trot—hides blushing
on the side of the box but it must go
with a different puzzle: our view
is an Oregon valley—or Alpine ski town—
not a cozy cottage in the sun:
where could we be on this card table?
Such mistrials, misfits. We're unable

to get it right—when all at once
like sitting for a photograph
the shoot is over. Here we are!
There's nothing more to do with it.
Leave it to be admired? Sometimes
in a thrift shop I'll find a jigsaw
glued to a board perhaps even
framed, now discarded when
another gewgaw replaced it
on some wall in a trailer park.
At last you lift yours, slowly.
Carefully break it up—shades
of the London Blitz or Ground Zero
—houses and towers plummeting into
their own shards, a mere fleck,
shred of the time it took to make

sense of them build them into
their final arrangement. Stir the pieces
scoop them back in the box; then up
with them to the high shelf until
the darkest week of another winter
when we feel defeated by
lowering, brief days. One morning
an urge, a nut to crack, a project
like cleaning out that closet
will loom on afternoon's horizon.
Any project to pass the time
will do on idle Sunday and we
begin to pine for another go
at solving a puzzle, the flowery
foreground of Anne Hathaway's
thatched cottage on a sunny day.

Shakespeare as Popular Culture

The vendors were universally challenged
or only vets who sat on their uniforms.

How stale to realize but the bard
was far off
like a mountain a frostie with mature
canopy of spruce and hemlock pastry motionless
at a distance
without a breeze marine.

It was time to stop hoping for a find
at that flea market—threadbare,
an empty barrel, mall of the new
with midges and the dumps
of dead stuff in boxes.
Nothing more post-Classical
or sweltering than this dry-streambed
moment in time. Your hair on end
as if grazed by lightning
and that provoked look in your eyes you
were about to strike out in Yiddish street talk
or military barks. *Nothing*
above bored here & precious little below.
Kvetch you later, elevator! How did
those Russian dealers get our number anyway
not our method but us
and our madness?

So we headed for home, eyeballs
drenched in tchochki; a road turtle
that almost slimed us bagged in the trunk.

The bar code seemed to be indicating B flat
but then it was time for Hollywood:

array of plastic Shakespeare place mats.
Get out of here you said to Anne
—of Green Gables by chance, or Hathaway—she'd
straighten us out all right; and teach those
hollyhocks a thing or two about
keeping upright not spreading
blooming and fuzzy by the fence.

The thatch will take care of itself
unless major weather burns it off
and that's not likely
here at the blissful roadside Softie Stand
where we've pedaled for the view
stopped cold in our tracks
by the gravity of the popular.

Flea Mart

Poor beggar loose and stiff at once
who had perhaps broken his back
sculpting his body, bent now as he
carried her packages, wearing only
leather shorts, Nikes, fanny pack.
Everyone saw each muscle pumping
beneath skin each fitting snugly
alluding to inner strength that none
who watched could see in the man who was
not young, not young. This was no time
aimed at the timeless his hapless trudge
dutiful behind her seemed to say—
and the burghers watching saw—how this
was no time or place for things to last.

Four Charcoals

Watching the men in fatigues half stripped
with girls in bras and shorts
unloading thousands of pounds of chalk
in hundred-pound bags
stacking them nearby

chalk to cover the dead the flood
and mudslide drowned in Venezuela was it
or Bangladesh

he wonders how best to feel cheerful
at the same time stricken. Beauty
queens and trustafarians
come together with survivors.

You try to be comfortable
but you've been there all day maybe two
sitting enough to get a sore butt.
You don't want to care anymore really can't, turn

to Seamus there on ITN in his Dublin study or kitchen
—what kind of space is it anyway?—saying *well
in 1985 I saw we couldn't have any more
elegies we'd had enough had to
turn to something different.*
You don't feel surprise anymore but
rejoice you can. Do. You can rejoice.

I get e-mail from you
instead of you. Maybe your voice

threw my neck out
trying to read it at a slant
while crying.—No I didn't but

truth is you've
forgotten me I can stand here
"forever" or decide
you don't matter and come out
of my coma—they once called it corner—fighting.
I guess you and lover are
somewhere murmuring playing a game
like Frisbee or Mah-Jongg. Only guessing.
Standing on the corner.
Waiting to leave my space.

It's not about heroes you know—
arma virumque—that's arms
and men and women too we know
but less epic than like Shakespeare's
history plays, a trail of finding
a new way relationships can work.

The mud buries thousands
flood drowns thousands
so many bodies lost forever
with no need of chalk; but
then.
A foreign country is sending water.

Emptying Air

Watching the day drift west
we looked for bats hunting
circling swooping to catch

their mosquitoes, gnats, flies.
They were a gift that swept
the sky—animals

each twilight combing the air,
the fields. Where were they what
now had happened? This morning

a chugging shudder wheeled,
long troughs of murmur now
returning, chuffing; bug-eyed

chopper sweeping hunting—
some trouble. Luckless gardener?
Child unaccountably lost?

The Baro

Ethiopia

It was enough to see him Olsen our photographer
  across the river waist deep
in sun-sheathed water. He stood leaning into the current
  for balance; a wake of chevrons
darks on brightness, trailing. I thought he stood on ledge
  that ran submerged near shore.
He stared upstream with fingers boxed as if framing
  a shot. This gave me pause.
When I looked up two minutes later he had gone
  no trace on the wide Baro.
Currents flashed like shattered windshields in sunlight. A braid
  of wavelets headed downstream;
we saw a chunk of weed trailing the prow of ripples.
  Impossible! He knew the rules;
no doubt he'd climbed ashore. Downstream we found a great one—
  the glasses showed our quarry
a rosy shred a flower at the jaw. McCutcheon
  stalked upstream tracked back
and paused in range downwind of turreted eyes. First fire
  missed then four shots more
at which the beast crawled down and under, vanishing.

Late Light

From cloudbank occasional shafts of sun scanned
calm seas and sand where tired ebb tide breakers
heaved nothing ashore. Fly fishermen out
from their campers dotted the line of water long
rods nodding seaward. Careful delicate
casts vanishing in gray light. Bending
rods reaching outward from anglers
like antennae of insects perhaps mantises
hoping for a catch but not having luck.

Then up the shoreline eddying in wash
to and fro lay the backbone and staring eye
of a striped bass, tail and spine with a few
stubs of rib. The silvered head as if smiling
with spread mouth that gasped not long ago.
Who or what I wondered made a meal of this
as it lay awash. Finished, shining in half light.

I asked the angler pausing to thread a fly
—what happened to the fish? He replied—that
bass? some guy out there caught him fileted him
threw him back for us to find and envy
or clean up—bastard messing with my shore.

Regime Change

Martha Kimbrough

An institution reconfigured, floor plan
to suit. Presidential restroom expanded
to accommodate the paying guests.
                              Time was
the Shah's daughter went to classes, skintight jeans
fixed smile half pout, dark eyes averted. Brace
of elderly bodyguards in madras slacks
smoking in vestibules. Limousine
discreet by flagpole. You still mopped classrooms
chucking ashtrays you once emptied.
                              That winter
Israel itching to bomb enrichment sites.
Snow blanketing old plumbing out the window
the tiled new space *wheelchair accessible.*
Outside, house finches at the finance officer's
squirrel-proof feeder.
                              Tour of duty over.
We're out. Weighted with cares for things gone by.

Guston's Crossing

Musa Guston

Then Philip Guston wept because the world
was going badly. He read the magazines.
He saw the cruelties, the brinks. Cliff edges

like the ledge great Peter's steed rears at not
knowing if he'll be spurred to leap or reined
back in. What could a painter do but go

"and adjust a red to blue"? There rose the heaps
of shoes. Their owners, dust. Now Peter's heir
removes a shoe to bang a desk and bellow

those threats to bury us all. Your father read
the graffiti on the wall. People didn't get it.
Where was the dream the elegant easel? Now

Nixon with platypus nose at San Clemente;
masked KKK men, sit-down comics; the naked
light bulb hung from its frayed cord—broad brush

bald scrawl casting his lot with ours. Dear Musa
you said you were going back to help while he
could work, making the next thing clear as he could.

Days of 1937

There on the mountain terrace where the lens
levels with snowcapped peaks those preened frocks
mingle with wing collars amid
attending uniforms smug with triumph.
      I watch the footage again

grandees obsequious, blustering generals.
One mote in their collective eye the lens
picks out a lad from the village far
below—believer or simply dull—
      bumpkin erect but frail

from a gleaming salver serving drinks head shaved
to vulnerable skull pale as a boy in Belsen.
Soon at the great rally a little
tyke in lederhosen runs after
      the leader—taken by guards

but not shunted away before the great one
turns back, arms wide as if to bless (discreet
applause from the crowd at such telling
concern). He is taking the child's scrap
      of paper is turning the boy

around; bending him over as if about
to punish leaning above him using his back
as a rest he is signing the paper: the crowd
adores the caper. In celluloid
      a past that ruler owned—

his splayfoot walk as if he strove to march
with earnest plucky strut, moustache like minstrel's

blacking—called up my father, gent
of 1937. I knew
              nothing of newsreels then

I knew looking up into his ruddy face
set with prickly moustache running to hug him
father home at dusk from the office
cold under the brushed grey homburg
              when he stamped in from the snow.

Little Night Music

Mozart was playing in my head this morning;
I wonder what was the dream it was adorning.
Yes someone's died. But I am not in mourning;

I met with the mortician thank god that's past.
And the tumor has not grown terribly fast
and I don't give a fig how long I last.

So daily a lot of Iraqis are dying in Iraq
and those warlike boys of ours are hearing the crack
of doom when homemade bombs pop up. At my back

time's shuttle over Acheron draws near
and slows for me—sinner as I am, in fear
of crossing over. The trip would come a cropper

but no matter. The mother of my days these days
is Mary Saint Mary mother Mary always
a refuge, Auntie Mary to whom I pray

buoyed and safe in faith, my castle, my keep.
What else to go for? Frame huger woes? Why weep
when I hear strains of Mozart and fall asleep?

Flight

He was not one to fly in dreams
but once while fast asleep he drove her
to the city that waited for him always
sunlit and still and welcoming.
They rode to a stranger's door to fetch
the potion a staring beggar had promised
would show them into the heart of things
into the very boulders where
old eyes sought out that sunlit world
like a filly in the open doorway
of her dark stall peering at noon.

But at the door where they inquired
the puzzled woman refused to help
would not admit she'd ever heard
of such as they were told to seek
but she served tea and bread still warm
at a table under an oak with leaves
that hung so low the tree would brush
their brows as if with wings as if
heavy with longing to touch their hearts.

Aubade

Dream the Flexible Intern went out saying
doctor will be with you in a moment.
Day and eyes opened to old light, that vamp;
the merriment of night slunk off.

He carried the project of insight sharp-shooterly
toward trouble.
                    Everything had gotten close—
electron microscopy of words revealed
just about anything. You named it you
bought it. He persisted like Camus peering
—though carefully appearing not to—askance
down the street called Scant. Go with it my heart!

Amped guitars scrawled lines across the ears.
Music of the spheres was like a worn brick
once ballast rising from tideline, oval baguette
sprinkled with sand.
                    Then wind gusts cuffed his loft.
In their casements windows knocked
like evangelicals intent on getting in.

Feed the World

His soil was rocky not the gingerbread those Czechs
bragged of. But he was glad for the gardeners
of Prague blithe folk far off; a life worth gardening for.
A squad of men ran past, thick thighs below sport shorts.
When they jogged back they paused. Their low voices
by his fence. He saw Greek bravos on an Attic cup.

They glanced his way and climbed into their sport
vehicles, mighty as the Trojan Horse. That hour
workout was enough to keep them fit, gird them
for days he thought spading where years ago
a road ran eight inches down. He had no prospects
but flowers would perform. In Prague men had

good dinners, vintage wines; on farms heat rose
from byres to sleepers—hooves below stamping
on straw. Still in the windy deserts of the world
men stood twisting, twisting. He turned the soil.
Road stones cropped up once more rose up like seedlings.
In another country, men were questioned to death.

Russian Dolls

He made do with a garden small as a tennis court.
When he'd started he thought of a soccer field. But hoping

for food from clay in three months' time was stupid.
His dream had been a truck farm without the truck.

A plot about the size of Ryoan-ji would do
with scholar rocks brought in from 25th Street.

At last it was scarcely larger than a game board
for Parcheesi. When you are olding less is not more—

hardly! But small begins to look all right
easier to transport by car or camel or knapsack.

The tailor sewed diamonds in the lining of her coat. Li Po
loved his land, moss on limestone. But he settled

for landscape in a tray. Hyman stowed his ancient
coins with drafts of *The Armed Vision.* The Nubians

okayed new towns but grieved for prior quays,
homesteads their forebears built. Lake Nasser rose.

Soon—forced resettlement. They filled their pockets
with soil from their native places when they trudged off.

Discovered Country

Sky dark, low, blunt as a boot; the last wild geese rendezvous on Flint's
Pond, glide into loud formation; mournful cries. Today we learned
of theft: Kenny's new shoes, books. Then food from the kitchen. Like a
bird when shot some life flew out of the wound—as quick breath hisses
from a punctured tire.

La beauté de la nature, said Landsman, *est le silence de Dieu.*

People shouldered their packs; made their way to their trucks.

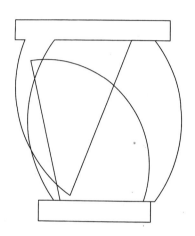

Inn of the Beginning Bar and Grill

The heat was merciless and it was on.
We could not recall how we had come so far
no destination but for slaked desire.
Look, distracted by distances destitute

in spite of credit we have no business here
and never gave a damn about permissions.
Taillights shimmer in smog of intersections
agents track us in the forbidden city

to a cul de sac where carcasses trundle on hooks.
We huddle while a leering worker chants
"you are about to have an industrial accident."
Suddenly as a backfire everything stopped.

We woke, kindly and affectionate; we saw
that time as if an accelerator would unleash us;
sensitive to our touch; our miles; our wish
here at the Inn of the Beginning Bar and Grill.

Nailed

There would be an end to it. The road a slick
dissolving in windy snow unreeling over

the nothingfields of Minnesota. Easy
to whack a person on because—tonight

where could he hide after the car one-eightied
in a drift prisms of snow going red? And he

a sweet guy after all, mouthing snow
like hope, pleading; just because he had

witnessed wrongful death. Well isn't any
death wrongful in this world of buds?

The New Job

No one has said a thing for twenty minutes.
I know it doubtless has nothing to do with an angel.

When I am eating snow I see how I fail
to realize my ideals. I hear hail on the roof

it's a bad situation. Lightning lances above me.
I know my happiness is not long for this world.

I hear a neighbor has been raped. Now I see distress
in every friend. When I am submissive I feel

like a recruit again—enduring the eventless life.
In a tunnel I see cavalry coming toward me

and know I am about to get a new job.
I look at my clothes brush and think of all the work

I have to do. I undress and know firsthand
how scandal and gossip cover my nakedness.

The ghost of my brother comes to the door. It says
you are in danger; do no business with strangers.

When a ghost speaks to me I know for sure
I am betrayed into the hands of my enemies.

Throws

In the machine, in the garden, the ghost wearing
the wideawake dropped by gypsies on the forest path
stared at us; inquired the way to Cragwood.
We had come from nowhere and had no answer.

The ghost had nowhere to go and fell silent.
At length it seemed to fade in the ivy and creeper.
One dream was to have a booth on the mountainside.
There you would pray to the light inaccessible.

After a time it would fold about you as a cloak
might gather. It would fall from the clouds lighting your way.
You would climb on upward stone after stone. Then
the sea, glinting beyond in ghostly light.

But you went down, losing the way, half running.
Legs would ache and body totter to reach
the level field. You found yourself on a midway
at a fair where children jostled against you.

You saw the maimed, my friend, outlined on tents;
played games of chance—a throw might win you a stone.

Triptych

Francis Bacon

Now where did that come from he wondered
where had he been the last
three days? And eaten? Had he
eaten anyone's star-date soup? At the
trenchers of Lahore?

It trickled down the left side for once, like porridge
but he didn't have the urge to scratch.
Still in theory he could nurse all his limbs
and moving them didn't make any pissant little sighs
noises like nutshells cracking or

hiccoughs deep within.
He had an array of disorders—like a lord's—
but they would pass, a 48-hour thing. Meanwhile
trucks beeped threateningly as they backed up
and the Hasidim driving them looked out

in their big fur hats like old Warsaw aristocrats
inspecting their fields from carriages
leaning from windows, smiling at the children.
Everyone smiled and drove each other, honorable
lightness of Poland.

My love is winging its way to you
announced the pop-up card that opened to an aerial
view of distant Manhattan. Never doubt it,
painter of blue sofas! Your message
on the other the cloudy side:

your most devoted and obedient servant.

So then. Now that we understand the weekend
is it easier to be dead in the country
or the city? We were just beginning to wonder
how long it takes to go through the pants and dipes.
You just start thinking about things while you're waiting

for the dryer.
Probably easier to be dead in the city
he opined but also easier to be alive
in the city—more Hispanic chances more tickets
more stuff on the curb. You get it:

his paintings show how it is—Sunday
mornings in a room of asthma. Or is that
the drawing room, mulish blues damp greens
a guy hanging out on the sofa looking up assignments?
We count too chortle the gerbils in their cage ripping

confetti. From a flounce among the dust balls
a little critter tiptoes on little feet
to a corner perfect for watching. In grimy fog outside
ravens scold about a spurt of vomit
in the gloaming under their tree.

Fable

On the seacoast in the stone
donjon of St. Margaret's
the lad in the iron mask
hurled silver dishes from
his casement window, costly
plate his captor (whoever
it was) gave him in their

invisible affair
to cosset him at meals;
silver from which to munch
his bread of idleness.
The boy in irons has
a fork, inscribes his pleas
in docile silver; flings them

out, bright circles spinning,
silver flashing in sun.
Grim syllables flying to light
the gleaming missives sailed
like Frisbees through the air.
Then down—to be scooped up
at dusk by a luckless drudge

weary from hauling nets
fisherman beaching his catch.
With manacles, with hosed
salt water and iron tongs
the jailer in his tower
soon satisfies himself
that the unshaven tar

bearing this chased silver
to the tower door is no

nautical swain out of
an eclogue who reads. Proves
beyond a doubt the brute's
unlettered, before he severs
the tongue and sends him home.

Denial

A man said Penelope was just in denial
that was all and we understood;
her inability to think it was him
after all those years; the test of the bed
consider all that business about
an olive tree maids hauling the mattress
outside her door for the poor guy.

Denial afflicts us all because
who wants to believe what has
happened happened and
nothing can be done even though
so many years have gone by and we
are completely different
and they are completely different.

He fought those battles and
lost his men again—and again
before losing his gear including
loin-strap and fleece jacket,
hardened himself to seductions
holding on through so many storms
sea salt in scrapes, limbs bruised blue.

Huang's *Tao Te Ching*

Scott Carino

How can you return the copy I lent you
when the book has vanished; flown relentless
as a Canada goose? Out there, Scott,
on the shadowy arc of Tao where
things pass unseen beneath our feet, our eyes
Huang's translation of the *Silk Text* is gone
to the nameless harmless he-man borrower
who thoughtlessly boosted it
while browsing the edgy insights . . .

"Stop your hole. Close your door."
—it said and you read it often—
"Soften your brightness. File your sharpness."
Harmless may be a good path
but with us uptown Western stragglers it's
bound to be a put-down. No threat.
Huang had just finished his literal

Tao Te Ching and was listening
to his favorite, Tommy Dorsey
when Mao's merciless gang
with clippers cut his thread.
Home from exile near Beijing he lies
in a grave beyond his work a half day's bus ride
from the prison that raveled his one life.

Two for Tu Mu

1

Old poet, lover of caves
inveterate seeker or, looking
into the sun setting
seeing a cracked mirror
where your rod crosses the swelling
disc, you bring to mind
slow Lincoln staring past columns

of his fascist-heavy temple
acropolis confining
a man; poet or hero, both
caught both alone. We get
to visit the basement now
we may think of Coleridge
spelunker of mind and giddy

pilgrim in Michael's grotto.
In the dripping cellar we watch
the marble leach in the Lincoln
Memorial basement, marshy
cellar pools at Potomac
water table coaxing
ghostly stalactites from stone.

2

Coleridge in a romantic Malta
chasm looking at thirty
women and boys doing
of all things—chores!—the washing
beating shirts, and the zoom lens
of his oneness-seeking eye

tracking the hairy "just
like a man" legs of a woman.

Amazed as Tu Mu in Chiang-nan as
threatened, man looking
with grappled-for courage and some
cheer at this lower-class
brooding, common, lower-case
spectacle of the beyond;
hankering after caves
pilgrim of cave and chasm

the notebook man with his pencil;
his minuscule sublime.

Adams in Japan

Lone herring gull stout with age
overweight as a slow day-tripper
stepping from a Boston ferry
patrols the shoreline surveying bathers
posed on the strand at polite distances

from each other. Flat feet, thin legs
should not support a body so
ungainly—in my gaze a dinosaur
survivor. In his, I am a creature
from another world or one from this

who may just leave morsels to scavenge.
As at Kamakura long ago
fishermen with nets it would
amaze to find a human bathing
in the sea unclean and dangerous sea

when Henry Adams—ponderous limbs
dripping—rose from the shallows. They
flocked to him, all speechless to touch
to contemplate this creature from
the sea; scrawny elfin fellows

browned, hardened by labor, reaching
to touch the pale barbarian
as he clambered into his delicate
black rickshaw to return to the city
one day in 1886.

Stones

Jane Hanks

From the porch eaves wisteria bloomed
like little clusters of twilight
the day I stopped to call.
You used to show me, out of the genial clutter,
perhaps a Thai carving or a bursting
lily cropped from the bright garden.
Now your rooms are
                spaces almost
echoing—spare, disrobed.
Bald sunlight through windows
pooling on blind-nailed floors.
Those boys of yours were dealt
dressers, upholstered chairs; your drafts
to libraries;
            old letters, bits of china to friends.
An envelope with your father's verses—English
for Christmas, Latin for spring—came my way.
You're almost ready to go now though the Keith
landscape stays on the wall above your grand
from California.
          The stones
rest in a Chinese rice bowl between us
brown like malted-milk balls
only larger more shiny more solid looking.
"Now take a few in your hand" you say
passing the bowl. I heft a couple,
chink them together.
            "You see, these mean
I've had good karma. All those years
in Thailand, in Yunnan. Never
a problem. Till now. But here I am."
You take your bowl back, eyeing me.
"Look here! I call these stones—my jacks."

Historic Preservation

The Chamber of Commerce had been at work. Father
pulled over to show his boys. A bank in Northfield
the Younger Brothers and Jesse James elected to rob
morphed with the years to a barbershop. Someone
had painted red circles round the bullet holes to show
where Northfield deputies took down the outlaw gang.

Later, he knew, they kept the robbers in a cave
with an iron door down by the river a limestone hollow
where cheese was cured on the banks of the Minnesota.
But that was an old man's tale. Eventually
they learned how James hightailed it back to Tennessee
leaving behind as the tintype shows the Younger clan.

They die as a camera shoots them slumped
in a row along the wall glass-eyed
like caught fish
pinned in the air now sweat-dark
shirts glinting with blood—
dumb guys stiffening pining to know.

Then he drove them to the banks of the Minnesota
showed how to prospect for the local fossil: bugs
a million years old with ridges like holster straps
or football harness. The creatures lay in the leafy shade
of hollows: embedded in shale huge trilobites
across the gully from cheese caves long abandoned.

Circular Drives

When I was a kid taken to the best end of the lake
the raked gravel of someone's circular drive
—always rustling evenly under the tires

with a hushed crunch—served notice, served privilege;
distant, esteemed. Maybe an Ordway's place
or the leaf-free drive and lawns of Southways

long and green in shade near private waters
where a dog or two dozed on a dock: where my father
inched the car forward to make his delivery

the low drum roll of pebbles decorously jostling
beneath us—surely heard behind the great
front door by someone waiting, or on guard.

Dealing, 1928

In the photo of my father dealing cards
five of him stare down each other. They
are all the one man. It's done with mirrors.
I might have known the one, but which semblance
should I have chosen, each with starched collar
dapper moustache, and the same hand? Each covers
for the others. Whoever they were, if he knew.

Possum

Because I made the promise twice
to wake him to say good-bye I barged
into the shaded room to rouse him
before I dressed packed went down
to meet my taxi for the airport.
It was no dream that I called out

and shook him gently in the dark,
robins starting to call in the gray
dawn the only other sound.
Wrapped in sheet and thermal blanket
arms crossed on chest Osiris-like
he lay in bed supine, stock-still.

Again I knelt and shook him; held him
but he slept on as in a trance.
All I could raise from him was a sighing
breath. My time was up. When I
closed the door a duck squawked once
to empty air down on the lake.

That night a thousand miles away
I fretted; phoned to say I'd tried.
Laughing he said he feared to tell me
how he had been awake but playing
possum—not up to saying good-bye.
This was no dream and I lay waking.

Rockhound

He turns the news off, takes his pail.
I watch him climb
the stream bed seasonal
but here now, up through the scent
of noon of timothy, on to the sandpits.

At glacial alluvial deposits
he scouts for jaspers and likely agates.
Father on the sandbank with his hand rake
claws a gravel acre
where dozers clank and grade nearby.

Eyes peeled
he'll uncover keepers and move on
while redwings and finches pour
choruses of being there
on half-deaf ears. Back home

he'll spill his pail, line up his darbs, choose
beauts to tumble grind and polish days
on end. He'll disregard the discord of the Cat
forget the news
keep his head down; keep his views.

Thrift at Christmas

Tom at 99

Herod says to Stephen, you are no more
able to be God's witness than this chicken
on my plate. Whereon the chicken lifts its head
and crows *Christus natus est.* Herod
sends Stephen to be stoned by fools
rabble Tom forever calls jack-asses.

Tom doubts yet keeps his promises—
tends friends, tends money. Says *I have
grave doubts of life beyond the grave.*
In a basket eyes of his potatoes crane
round to the sun at his window where
beyond is winter, a zero at his smile.

Ladybug

The new ladybug is huge, not trig
like the natty ones we knew once. Still
like their kin—harmless hemispheres—
they do laps, shy dabs bright with color
lightly zooming at windows. They glow
like poppy petals straying aloft
or quicken bowls of nasturtium on sills.
But look at them now. Octobered

they wait to revive in sunlight.
No longer in orbit they sit as if
on verandas; grow grayish, scarce
awake until their papery bodies
white now and flightless roll away
not fit to give color to the world.

Jumble

Who would have believed that jet
necklace Great Aunt Clara wore
Victorian mourning gesture for
her doctor husband who disappeared
Eugene on a midnight patient-call
in newly settled Lake Mills Iowa—
black chunks of flashing beveled jet—
was only the petrified
wood of the monkey puzzle tree?

Or that Cecil Rhodes that lout
hustled the tale that scam about
diamonds being rare. Started
the fad for huge engagement rings
such as Eugene sweated for
and bought his Clara. Her diamond
thought a rarity she wore
pacing her floor murmuring love songs
of Heine. Her steps half mincing half
the confident walk of a gentleman
on his forest floor stalking a deer.

Sweet Corn Next Right

1

A lot of people are standing around
waiting to tell you stories. Their
stories. Or so they say. You say
take them with a grain of salt. Sincerity
recall is in the mind of the beholder
this afternoon. Often has been. You hear tell.

Watch out for adoption placement scams
and those up-trou cams suspended in
shopping bags, ladies making rounds
doing their job, getting the shots we
ordered silver box shooting while
you wait for the woman to tell her story.

2

I admire that jimsonweed, it grows wild
anyway and—and in my garden too.
You know the little row I hoe.
Come over some afternoon after Diane
has been here with her bugle to get
whatever are eating the choice leaves.

She provides an air of risk and mystery
to devil-may-care gardening on the edge. As for me
allow me to say those white trumpets at teatime . . .
such blooms! But I still prefer the bassoon. I promise
not to use it architecturally, or on the
campsite. Honest, I'm that serious.

Toward Perfection: A Practical Treatise

Magenta girl with azure face
and palms of purplish hue embraced
by clouds of apricot and pink
play rusty violin in space
sealed by lemon wimpling prink
of daffodils whose interlace
coagulates like frothing drink.

If this be so—that an old case
was used—well you should replace it
with a better year, or paint,
than this—alas, my lass.

Pentimento

The water was satisfactory but
old pipes would knock. Soon rusted
grunge came out; he paid and had
filters put in. He thought a lot—

he wanted her there as he did of old.
But iron in flakes rose up the pipes as
fast as it filtered out it was
always there. From a street washed gold

at sundown, abrupt alarm of a car
climbed to his floor; abruptly lost.
Silence. He caught a scent of exhaust,
of ache and pain, under the door.

Sixes and Sevens

He was suddenly terribly tired
and decided to go to bed.
He hadn't lost at golf or been fired
yet something was up in his head.
He saw his love was estranged
and a tired heart grow surly.

He had every detail arranged—
he dreamt it all—he would get up early
go back to work. *Labor is life*
it said on the postage stamp.
What he ought to do was surprise his wife
comfort her in a parking ramp

in the dank of the echoing sodium light
in the car by now they nearly owned.
But again he felt a gust of fright.
And again the fervent stranger phoned.

A Dance

The Sistine Jehovah reaches to touch Adam.
And so the boy's body will touch his grave.
A crow made cries, sounded his horn, his warning.

We don't know why the wall did not crumble.
At last the suture heals and the child will live.
Clouds pass overhead and his life is happy.

He can believe he rules the night. Those years
are like a tuber's tendrils questing in the cellar.
It will be years of keeping up before he sees

before the thing of it dawns one afternoon.
Sculpting the body is for stars. The Milky Way
makes a cincture over the muscled belly.

The soul was like a tiny Aztec dancing
above his head not sure which way to fly
now that the trunk and limbs had given out.

The finger pointed and grazed the marble shaft.
The stone made a wall between him and his love.
He understood but with a veteran dismay.

Veil

A veil of Bach from a box
as from shaded windows. A woman
from Hospice bending over
the rail of the rented bed
hands clasped as if in prayer,
her calling of grief. We feel
we do intrude on this
lone space our Hannah busy
breathing; clenching eyelids.
A moment of brief calm
as of waking all at once
from fierce crowdings of a day.

Of anomie, of fractal sameness
when dense crowds uncoil
in hasty fracas to a loud
concourse of departures;
of clatter like crashing glass
as a train brakes to a stop
hissing. So the pilgrim
on the stairs has not a minute
to cool her heels or heart
waylaid among gadgets
that seem to save. Yet only
her savvy works today.

Rising belly where the crab
like a sea lion on his shore
too overweight to roar
holds in the morphine dusk
hours ticking, ticking.
Like mosquito gauze
drawn over the sluggish room

ponderous scent of lilies
curtains the knower, one
corner of that lip blue
in the precinct now of Bach.

Terra Nova

Go to the garden gray with granite cobbles
where daisy, fern and dusty miller wince
in sun, where indolent lilies lean and bud.

Go down the footpath to the blue-walled pool
where excellent MacCulloughs plashed and swam,
blank to the sky as the crater of a bomb.

Dry the pool, dry concrete edged brown.
This is their dust; and yet aloft stained glass
in the vast cupola—where long ago

MacCullough's children laughed and cried with joy—
blooms in the sun at noon this noon that comes
to wipe each shadow from deserted walls.

Spell

A letterhead with architectural shield
of Brown's Hotel Denver Colorado,
the graver's lavish flourishes long grimed
by fingers. Across the sheet on a dusty field
of Crane's best stock handwritten letters stood
unwobbling. Stood like fence posts in the snow,
like gate posts and their gates. The linked strokes climbed
to make a gaunt design I could not read
at first. Cyrillic? Saxon? Inches of ink
drew slowly up and down as if beseeching
meaning to come. They spelled—H E L E N K E L L E R.
I felt the hand that rallied there upreaching
toward the pace of light; the all but interstellar
tracings. Calculations on a field else blank.

The Field Glasses

Like a stalling film projection, the hummingbird
sips at bee balm—pause—at hosta—pause—
bee balm. Another pause; it vanishes.
Then it is there again at a bittersweet
tendril hanging.
              I bought him field glasses
in Tokyo, upmarket pair with zoom lenses;
father retired, happy on Mount Curve.
He kept them by the window, focused for evening.
One couple now and then forgot to draw
the blinds late hours across the way. Father
had much time! Now where his eyes pressed

to scan those two I scan hosta, bee balm.
A hummingbird, now two, in the honeysuckle
alight then mount in dance above the flowers,
helix of flashes; impalpable animals braiding
air, unaware of pleasure they might give.

New Place

To be there; to understand what it was
before us. To see the weathervane idle
at dawn beyond the cedar branches
or now on flanks of dunes in wind
salt spray on rose-bank; and the ivy
poison to us. You tread between
their networks parting rose and rose.
Peering with caution or expectation

you go at the ready for what must be
the sound of the hammer a neighbor wields
stranger you have no fear of yet
you don't know how his lingo goes.
You two shake hands; then one turns back
to work—for a moment studies the hand
that's lately been in yours as he turns
to nailing the old clapboards and the new.

Names for Birds

—So many birds are still here for us
    and their names. Juncos pine
siskins loud relentless jay remind us
    how little we get to choose
when it comes to a touch of color on grayest days
    —or in a cove by the sea
the swan and its cygnet. Again the finches
    now and then egrets;

we talk we argue over what might be
    the proper name for this
fisher of elvers on watch motionless
    at nightfall on granite coping
of stream wall cormorant or junior heron
    —then at high tide come
morning no one is up but one to see
    the Great Blue by the window

none but one to verify and name.
    So many creatures have
names for us to divide the world up into.
    So much more to be named
than Adam who had no concern to separate
    lion from jaguar civet
from house cat. Animals without voices
    to whom we give each a

label we imagine gives a being—
    a voice—as new citizens
register at polls and make thereby
    a presence known. I watched
an animal watching me as it showered
    under the sprinkler between

the dwarf false cypress and a lady's-mantle
    I peered at it and watched

in the failing light and thought it peered at me
    but it was only a clod
in shadow. I'd forgotten the remains
    of digging I had done:
possessed of neither name nor motion no
    creature yet it seemed
to watch as if hunting. Tufts of sod
    like ears curled aloft

listened through the swash of water but
    it was nothing. The mistakes
were mine. Yet I had to ask if having names—
    as swans do this strong-necked cob
paddling to command with calm pen keeping
    tabs at tideline on two
cygnets—accounted for their being there
    knowing it was not so.

North by Northwest

Auburn as dusk like the windless grain
I saw him prance in the sown chosen
field like Homer's fox stepping

in snow, alert in haste. Above
from my black window I would not
have spotted him that hazel coat

against Montana boondocks blond
in the sun alone at our right-of-way
had Homer's painting not come to mind—

mind steadily scrolling. The fox
with his groomed brush waiting there
in the tumult of Amtrak's Express.

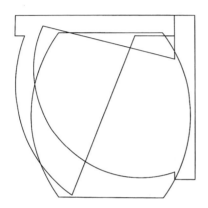

The Players

Through rain one night I drive twelve miles.
A darkened hall where country actors
are about to play Molière
as they have done O'Neill Chekhov Shakespeare
for more performances than they remember.
Now to encounter Nevin's interpretation

of the miser hypercrafty Harpagon
part villain and part fool; his other life
"licensed nursing assistant"—paying job.
So Kim who plays Frosine the go-between
has her day job too. All of them live
to live again their parts: the boy actor

Jason now the man Valère has his career
with local engineers. He loves his role
and plays each swagger and alarm of smiles
lost in himself. Each fathoms free delight.
They find an alien welcome meaning
in their parts voices they hear as well as speak.

Tonight these give starry meaning to hard
nursings; words from memory called up
that they rejoice to say. Lines from that reticent
chamber closed in the head cross over and out
changing the night for players into something
like meaning; like enchantment manifest.

Landscape with a Storm

Poussin

We take in these Poussins—room after room;
green more green; green hills—how rarely thunder.
Where we wonder is frost; the naked branch,
sere leaf? How is it—outside against the wind—
that snow stares down from skylights bright with day
perfecting light that swathes these canvases
with color? We know—we know it's only art
these rooms carefully hung, compelling beyond
assent. Beyond your keenness to embrace
what you're on watch for. What do you see watching
the oxen kneel before the coming storm
their driver crouching in crimson smock now
salaaming before the darkness the coming roar?
It's nothing but the weather we infer
latecomers to this painter's sumptuous world.
Here is no one's sorrow not bravery tethered
with frailty, joined for no one's sake. The picture
seems to urge the trembling man to rise.
To get those oxen off their shins and up
off the ground; on with their journey to deliver
the cargo someone waits for. But each of these
astounded creatures and the awestruck driver
huddles humbled, benighted
                                        —unlike the palace
towering on a cliff beyond that no storm touches
in sunlight still. We find a bench and sit;
looking here, dry passengers; a gallery at noon.

Constables at Auction

IMPORTANT CONSTABLE

The canvas showing Stoneleigh House. Well dressed
with terraces. Round these, gardens, fields.
There in the middle distance thatch-gray hills.
In sky of Wedgwood blue clouds hover at rest

on craggy matrix earthen world that yields
to mower sheaves to gardener room for frills
—a dial of roses for time that turns alone
wheeling in darknesses no master owns.

PEN AND WASH SKETCH

A canvas showing Appleton House
and round it gardens, pastures, fields.
In the middle distance scumbled hills
frame tiny field hands and their ploughs.

The composition's foreground yields
Damon the mower with his scythe
and song; and the head gardener with
his sundial, flowers for Time alone

floating down wells where galaxies spill
an acreage no man may own.

SCHOOL OF CONSTABLE

The sheet of Kempsford House
with crosshatched field and garden.

He is walking out of doors
whom everyone obeys

each man each maid at chores.
Beater and dogs flush grouse

earning the timely pardon
of his lordship's hunting gaze.

Jerome

Rembrandt

My cell's next door where Guilty died, or summer
drills its seed. Green-fisted master! that bully
sun tugs flowers and I a dusty drummer
trudging earth's dusty drum tug fitfully.
I'm webbed with burs—a hex on this burdocked plexus!
—thistle and mud-cake sneeze from the broom a gnu
in a nursery ABC.
               Yet I weave this nexus
of threshing thorn to flesh of me and shoe
my toes with kisses.
               It's pudding unloading the cloth
for God. While Leo mouths flies and tends the flocks
I pen the trot. He meets the household brunt
(while I muse wisely; doze; or let my moth-
delighting taper baste its friend, or the phlox
grow pale, or sandal-lapping Leo hunt).

Sewing Bird

When he worked in Madrid
restoring the paintings of the Baron
I knew he was thinking of home
the refrigerator door ajar
bottles inside chinking a little together
glowing in the low-watt light behind them
as he sat down at the table
thinking about odd things like spoons
that he could grip hard without fear
and hold in his fist.

He studied the little pocks of the sewing bird
on his work table with its pot of ballpoints
little track of dents running round the edge
left by a housewife wearing a tippet
who needed another hand as she sewed;
and the irregular chain of notches
cut by a schoolboy's penknife.

I thought of him hurtling through Europe
on a midnight express
past fields with small harvests people like him
made to find themselves
a latter joy, the closing suture.
On that midnight express
he gazed out the cold window
at his kitchen table warm and lamplit, tucked
in the granite hills of Vermont.

Tom in the Taconics

The racket made him think he had a flat.
The warning sign said GROOVED SHOULDER. Then
flashing electric display—WATCH FOR FALLING
ROCKS. His lane an obstacle course, chert blocks
and trucks at hand.
                    Always a surprise in wait—
as when the clivias opt to bloom, stiff columns
rising with hardly a warning in his room
and soon their domes of blossom pulsing orange.
Wheeling into the canyon of living rock
scooped clean he felt like a giant hurled
down with plummeting rocks as in Salvator's
etching of titans.
                    He threaded into the cut
someone's heavy equipment carved; he passed
oncoming vehicles. How better than a farm
was anyone's guess, he thought—this motorist
whose mother was in service whose father kept
a tractor oiled and furrows straight—and saw
how business boomed below a field that was.

Side Hill Farm

He mowed those seven acres left now his pair
with cutter bar pulled through the summer making
a kind of lawn of what was once a field.
The buildings stood, or what was left of them;
a roof, a crib would snap and sag; soon enough
each one would list until it fell. The docks
for loading logs remained like the hulls of ships
beached on a hillside. Boys to the city gone
and men to Holden's Mill down hill in town.

No fume of gasoline but cries of crow
and shape of hawk shadowed vole along
the field he mowed out of a lingering care
for those days, black rotted lumber ramps
behind a scrim of wild cucumber, bush clover.
The owner died and family moved, acres
to corn gone fallow. No reason to hold on
up here where no one meaning business came
but maybe on an afternoon picnickers
would hike their way up Glastenbury ledge
to use his field, warm faience-green about
to be buried in long plots of underbrush
and popples getting started. Woodchucks found it;
hillocks of earth rose at their tunnel doors.

But now they file to hedgerows, lilac and such
where loggers built their little hamlet; dig
in deep. Before the season closes down
they have advanced to take positions in cellars
of houses left to tumble; out from under
they climb to graze, pause there waiting listening
to the grind and thump when he at twilight back
from work down valley cuts the owner's field

rough clumps of grass smoothed out until a trim
lawn comes round again for him; and the budged
woodchucks watch, make do with what's at hand
munch to bursting, stay on and do not care.

Wheel

Now how much longer the road is though
it is the same road he needed to take
for years. He needs time he never
took or had the patience for
the day is longer now and now
he has an inkling that feels right.
He has no one to drive but himself

and here it is carefully signed in blue
REST AREA, one of the last lay-bys
not closed not barricaded from us
for drug deals sex or some such crime.
Under maple and alder birdlime
on picnic tables; nearby a spot
by the state's chain-link fencing not
dense with glint of poison ivy.

A place he can go in peace—then back
to the table forgetting the screened highway's
keening whirl. He watches a man
pee where he peed. Now from the bowl
cradled in a Ziploc of ice cubes
the bisque she made him. Tart. Red.
He spoons alone in the shade—shade
cooling his heels—his wheels—the day.

Candles

When the war came that year it was the fashion to place
a light in the window then lights went on each night to give

some shape to a dark that rose from the streets a flood swelling
with fear while they waited for reliable news from the front.

A candle or electric holiday light that looked like a candle
showed you supported the troops showed you were *on board*

perhaps even a parent of one out there and you
honored their loved ones of course and were opposed to war

and prayed this one would soon be over. In the event
few fell if thousands of enemy perished slowly triumph

broke out over the city soon candles winked out as when
a parade has passed and the music fades—though in one window

a light burned on long after the war was history. What
did it mean who lit it each night that far watch fire burning.

Cold Thicket

Old straw
for warmth back then
manure

to burn back then
what food only
hot nettle soup

burning our hands
to gather
newsprint

books anything
for heat
the hardest time.

Nothing. Black
market farmers
hiding a few

potatoes out
from troopers
everywhere

on roads who
requisitioned
took stole *took*

everything grown
that was not
hidden. He

needed to
barter *and* eat
his little trove.

Supposed to last
they—they! said
only a month or

a year but it is
always, when
you hunger & thirst

and time is not
what you said back then,
your "mercy

of eternity"
in a hungry
frozen world.

Amarna Relief

Akhenaten

The young pharaoh lifts an olive branch
in a delicate hand, reaches for sun whose rays
caress it with tiny fingers. Thus, fragility.

The text at upper right is hacked away.
We cannot know but guess. Ignorance of things
shelters frailty. Thus our guess—lucky

like a young ruler who could not know how soon
his faith would be obliterate. It would be cut
from the stones of his body where the arm rises

to hold the branch to sunrays, fruitful Sun
—those blocks men hauled to make their temple
so many thousand cubits from his prayer.

Sea Chest

In the junk shop stood an old wood chest
patina of ships and the sea, use and years;
the box heavy empty forgotten set apart.
On the lid stenciled in bulky black a sort of tattoo
the legend read JOHN SLATE / LIVERPOOL.
He wanted to ask but never found out, was Slate
out of Liverpool or *bound for* it? Down one end
small letters read *E. S. Liverpool.* Is that his son
or did that have to be another? Watch by the sea
he thinks, stand there till an aura grows clear like
some maritime koan, or a bottle frosted and cracked
holding a slip of paper, riding the tide.

Fourth Dimension, Etc.

Only the challenged do not know
how time like a traveler ant
with dishes for the queen
is bearing them briskly away.

Feeling they lean on something more
leaves both of them a slice
of respite then one forgets and soon
again forgets—in spades this time

his debt to pay. Ignorant to think
he spends a bit—a weekend or a week—there:
eternity that feckless wallow
where time would never wander.

As Smoke Robes Fire

Ben Belitt

1

Creak on floorboards,
steps in the next room.
            Floorboards groan in mine.
I am an old man in office

positioned to observe.
            The time-lapse, the achieving:
no concern of mine. I enjoy
certain rights.
These, my defense.

2

Below, he hears voices, cars revving to go and
they go.
Or: cars return, people
bandy greetings sweet
nothings of some who are not
friends but have "quaint" acquaintance

The hum wafts the day to him

a sadness—as through torn upholstery
of ancient easy chairs
the stuffing rises

3

Sound of motors along the bay
CDs on deck throbbing the beat
to shore, while off Block Island

the whale heaves crusted back
above the waves. He feels
it has not been well for a long time

yet there it goes rising there
in sun, doing its life.
Mother of earth, of sea, dive deep—

4

Lonely men, men alone
smoke in the rain, Italianate
memorial tower scarved in spotlit mist.

Women in pairs
hold to each other, shelter, step
doggedly for home.

What is it by my bed
when the floor whines?

5

From bed taken to burning
worrying drifts of flashlight scrawls
melting on walls of light.

Flames assailing a city,
among shadows he pivots
peering
leaving behind a wakened after-image,
her parish of fire.

Cries at the shifting edges

strange tents of flame
drawing torn dreams together;

        sleep
only an ash hurtling in back-draft.
They chafe hands
    or reach out.
Reeling, the flames leap back.

6

Once more peace has been declared
once more civility decreed.

You have told me again
once I believed you
once I believed in you

Always the great pleasure
was coming home
eyes dazzled by colors of walls
flowers in warm light.

7

The card he sent paints Jesus
showing hungry people
the pizza he provides

Tibetan gurus
hid their teachings
for any and all
deserving to find them

Where am I? Who are you
whose steps sound on my floorboards?

8

Your journey, those lines—.

Positioned to observe, you studied
the Alps "that tiara of peaks
for a storm-king" beyond
the high balcony at Serbelloni.

Your journey—
your lines

left in obscurity by the glare,
chic themes on Disneyed shores—

like an animal's:
at sun-washed noon
one takes his stroll

sniffing about hillsides
to numerous and
signifying nooks he knows.

No one goes with him
the jaunt forgot
even by himself, yet it

is marked in grasses for another
to take the very walk
another day.

White Space

Nimbus of bees and flies halo the gold
    pot of asters he gave

before they left bright by flagstones marble worn
    as if of Rome. But this

was only their place; they were home. Still the cough
    from lock-up plane's

sealed air. Jetlag; tall grass, blue loosestrife,
    daisies. Jay and crow

out of ancestral branches guarding calling
    doing their drill. How

strange, nothing had moved!—and she
    on target, calling the cat.

Restive

Scooping out soil to plant he tugged
at roots refusing to give—those ropes
uncompromising held their ground
gridlocked only for him it seemed;
his spade, blade bright with sky above.
He dug and felt no strain to speak of,
muscle working on tendon but thought
those cables must be tugging back
from crazy angles, wanting their lanes.
A few were thick as a wrist yet some
were filament feeders for him to tear
disjoin and loosen. He wrestled them
this way and that. At last they gave.
At dawn in his room he feels them now
in his shoulder and his back. They tighten
against him while outside a dove
is holding its throat open to cool
morning, telling the trees, *now, now.*

Seriatim

The corridor
    where his smile
        had
    for so long
failed to apply.

Going the other
    way he met
himself on the beach
    and said

Come along with me
    and look down
into the floor
    of this matter.

Wind turns
    the fan in its socket
it chuffs
    though the power
        is off.

Seeing It There

The unconditional event
of hillside its fan-tracery
of oak and maple pulling sight

inward one October noon.
Nothing special you remark,
as nothing is. Reliably

itself that hill. Such colors. Must be
how someone "long in city pent"
beholds a countryside when he

cannot go there. To *not* come
upon it; sight not sharpened, focused
so much as warmed.